MORNING WATCH

MORNING WATCH

Meditations by
Barbara Pescan

Skinner House Books
Boston

Published by Skinner House Books, an imprint of the Unitarian
Universalist Association, 25 Beacon Street, Boston, MA 02108-2800.

Printed in Canada.

ISBN 1-55896-376-6

10 9 8 7 6 5 4 3 2 1
02 01 00 99

FOR ALL MY TEACHERS

CONTENTS

FIRST FIRE

High above you the sun shines
and beyond its glory
the stars of night
hide in the daytime sky.

Below your feet
worms
out of their bodies remake the soil
and at the center
the earth still simmers
with its first fire.

Somewhere
between the stars and the earth's core
we live
and weep
we ask
and laugh
and answer.

How can we not be amazed?
Let the light and darkness
bless each other   and bless us.   Amen.

LENTEN PSALM

My life has become
    a tattered rag I use
to drag across surfaces
dusty with dry sins.

I would wash it in the blue green lake
hang it to dry on a budding branch
pin it to the cuff of my sleeve so
whatever I lifted my arm to do—

working, praying, reaching,
lifting my arm above myself
my sullied self—

this rag would wave
flick through the dull air
    the bright air
    the holy, waiting air
in praise.

CALLING

Mother shaman—shake me
shake my bones, my certainties—
I am your fox tooth rattle—shake me.

Dance with me
pound my stretched skin
    inside outside
make me ring and make me tremble
I am your round bound drum singing—lift me.

Blow through me
across my eye holes
in my ear folds
blow the truth down my dark hollows
I am your horn
Your ram's horn mouth, mother—breathe me.

Old mother, come. Ahh.
Old mother, come
    dance me
    shake me
    sing me
    whole.

FOR SAPPHO'S SISTERS
AT FERRY BEACH

The laughter
spills from the women's workshop room
unbound guffaws
cascading peals
erupt from the windows
billow over the common
roll down the dune
to the roiling water

hot yuks
meet the tide
wave for wave
the ocean
slaps her knee
with one wet hand

Mother loves it
when we laugh.

MAMALIGA MUSCLES

My people make a dish out of rough ground corn:
mamaliga is water, corn meal, and salt
brought to a boil in a heavy pot,
simmered and stirred with a long wooden rod.
The mush gets thicker and thicker
becomes harder and harder to stir.

Frumosa fata, my grandmother said
pinching my cheeks, then pulling me to her,
holding me in her arms—
Beautiful girl, and so I felt whole and good in that
    embrace.

And ever since, my life, getting thicker,
has taken more effort to stir, getting the lumps out early
careful that the bubbling stuff doesn't burn me
my shoulders and wrists aching, holding on to the
    stirring rod.

God, am I done yet?
May I stop stirring?
May I serve up myself just as I am
turned out in a loaf

with butter and cheese on top
cut with strong thread in lovely slices of me
to family, friends, and all who
want a taste of this good food?

Frumosa fata, once,
I remember the gift of being seen as good
and beautiful for no reason at all.
I still am.
And, now, I am strong, too.

for my mother, Mary

Frumosa fata   pretty little girl

LISTEN

Those ratcheting mumbles of birds before dawn—
they are for us, too—
echoes of our own querulous questions.

Who are we?
Does anyone understand our suffering?
And how shall we find our voice
to keep singing songs of joy
when fear prowls at the boundaries of our lives?

Love comes and goes
loneliness visits too often
death will come humming our names
but for now
    for now
in this time full of day, of swelling buds
we, too, utter a song
though the meaning may be a mystery
along with the universe still murmuring its first sounds
we, too, sing

I am.

HOLDING IT ALL

Thou

I smile when I say it
Thou   meaning all that is
inside me   and   outside me
sometimes a tree
sometimes mountains
or the running doe
or the leaping heart
     of a finch held between my palms
or a child's hand, no bigger than a tulip flower,
     with no space in it yet for fear
     resting in my own.

Thou
that listens
to our tentative and doubting dreams
Thou
hear us into certain song
how we are touched
by the lives of our neighbors and kin
by their sorrows, healing, and hopes

In a silence we carry with us
all day long we whisper the names
of our people broken and healing,
with us and separated,
struggling and reborn

May we all be held by someone,
by something

Something like
hands
enfolding the pulse and flutter of a bird
Gently. Carefully. And slowly opening.

Thou. Let it be.

PRAYER FOR THOSE
GATHERED IN WORSHIP

In this familiar place, listen:
to the sounds of breathing, creaking chairs,
shuffling feet, clearing throats, and sighing all around
Know that each breath, movement, the glance
meant for you or intercepted
holds a life within it.

These are signs
that we choose to be in this company
have things to say to each other
things not yet said but in each other's presence still
    trembling behind our hearts' doors
these doors closed but unlocked
each silent thing waiting
on the threshold between unknowing and knowing,
between being hidden and being known.

Find the silence among these people
and listen to it all—breathing, sighs,
movement, holding back—

hear the tears that have not yet reached their eyes
perhaps they are your own
hear also the laughter building deep where joy abides
despite everything.
Listen: rejoice.   And say Amen.

A PRAYER IN FEBRUARY

Dearest Lover, Only One, You, Sweet Holy One,

last week it was 40° with sun and without
and we asked the trees not to forget themselves
in one loose moment's warm embrace with you.

We are impatient
and would not have the leaf buds swell
only to be surprised by one of your betrayals.

You
love in the bud, come.
I am moving slow as sap toward you—
bundled like a three year old
snow blind and laughing
I slide toward a pratfall into your lap—
giddy from chasing you
in all your wanton moods.

Oh, let me look at you
see you however you come
You, trickster   You
crystalshining bootslide   You
childfaced snowballer   You

You
know I keep on loving you
in spite of everything.

SOMETHING BEYOND TROUBLES

What I thought were snail tracks
silver in the grass
were instead
tinsel in short bits.

While my lover struggles
hard to hear her power,
I sit here with sister oak
her shade skirt scattered with tinsel
a dry leaf sighing across my lap
and the breath of God
up my back.

PSALM OF JOB

I have seen you in your creation:
in the wings of the hawk . . . her flight . . .
And I see how you walk
    the boundaries of the waters,
I have seen you in all good and gentle things.

I have seen you in the boils
    on the soles of my feet;
I have heard you bellowing
    in the heaps of dying animals;
You cry my name
    from the rubble where children are buried.
I have cursed you and demanded your answer—
You have been silent.
And yet

I cannot turn my gaze from you.
Though my eyes are dry in their sockets
    and tears will not come;
Wherever I turn my face to avoid you
    there you are.

I rage. I call your name.
And I hear your answer—
in the parched grasses bent to the hard earth
in the fire that eats and spits out burning char.
You are an absence, your name is all that is left behind.
Yet I look upon you.
I know I cannot turn
from the place where last I saw you.
I will search the face of the void.
I will continue to ask.
For this question is all I have,
this   and my eyes
which seek to see you face to face.

From a midrash on Job, for Harry Scholefield.

PSALMSONG

Ruah, breath of God,
spirit of creation
zephyr-kissing flowers
wind-tossing sequoias
hear me speaking to you.

We know the price of resurrection—
let us be willing, even knowing
that death comes first, to be reborn.

Rebirth is not only golden grace and glory,
it is labor and that first searing breath.

We know what exists in this world
and we choose to live
for this world is flowers and tears
it is blood and song.

Give us the courage to be resurrected
again and
again.

Oh, Spirit, kindle in us the passion
        to live with our whole self—
eyes open, ears hearing, nerve endings electric,
tasting and seeing and breathing
the fire of the indwelling spirit.

Ruah, breath of God, breathe us alive,
        with fear and hope and
Let us arise and
Let us arise   rejoicing !   Amen.

EASTERING

Why this sadness toward spring?
Half smiles at the first yellow flowers,
Tears pooling for no reason with each rain and sunset?

Each year this green show
blows wide winter's coverings and lets us see
the swell and push of beginning again.

Am I meant to rise too?
To push away what leans against the door of my
        pinched heart?
I cannot.
    Compassion for myself
    is a slow growing crop,
    however carefully tended
    it yields an unreliable harvest.

These resurrections
ask more than I can give
every time
this hurts more
than the pains of my body

than the old world full of sorrows
this offering of love
this unbearable gift of another chance.

WHO ARE WE AT EASTER?

Who are these who sing Alleluia
and call risen, risen, indeed
one
dead long ago
whose words are so often amulets
against the necessary struggles

as if any words alone could:
love against all odds
sing with the lunatic
reveal the nakedness of power
deliver the dispossessed to choices again
turn hope's prism for the blind to marvel
smooth hard places into feather beds for the broken
wrest from nothing and no way
the chance for children to grow whole
stretch easy the backs that bear the work
bless all the world with our lives
lived forgiving, alert for love

What fools, indeed,
who may never even discuss divinity
or agree on how much room there is anywhere
    for angels, again, to dance
but who
in their ancient poetry
with its curious syntax   and
in their reckless yearning insist
insist
love never dies
survives after the grave   even here
and claims us   yes, now
and will not ever let us go.

For my aunts and uncles.

MEMORIAL DAY PRAYER

Spirit of Life
whom we have called by many names
in thanksgiving and in anguish—

Bless the poets and those who mourn
Send peace for the soldiers who did not make the wars
but whose lives were consumed by them

Let strong trees grow above graves far from home
Breathe through the arms of their branches
The earth will swallow your tears while the dead sing
"No more, never again, remember me."

For the wounded ones, and those who received them back,
let there be someone ready when the memories come
when the scars pull and the buried metal moves
and forgiveness for those of us who were not there
for our ignorance.

And in us, veterans in a forest of a thousand fallen
        promises,
let new leaves of protest grow on our stumps.

Give us courage to answer the cry of humanity's pain
And with our bare hands, out of full hearts,
with all our intelligence
let us create the peace.

SHE SPEAKS OF DEATH

Oblivion, she said
in a weary voice,
is what is after death.
>   There is nothing after death
>   but nothing
>   and that's all right with me.

It made good scientific sense,
nailed to the cathedral door
of her religious childhood.

And when her husband died
a few years later
oblivion
pinned against eternity
sagged in the middle
and in its folds
sweet disbelief surprised her
and the hope
she hadn't seen the last of him yet.

For J. V.

RESURRECTION

He would not speak of death
banned all talk of it
but one day—
standing at the window,
white haired, elegant, composed
looking out at the yard,
at the chair near the hedge
where on soft afternoons he sat in the sun

—Yesterday I was thinking, What's the use?
Then, from inside the hedge a bird
hopped out to the end of the twig
perched for a long time looking at me
    then flew away over my head.
And then this came to me,
But, oh, it is all so beautiful—

His voice only a little softer than usual
amazing him
in acknowledging so much.
He turned from the window and sat down.

I wish I could say
I said nothing more
No, I said too much and was not asked back
did not see him again until, on his death bed,
he could not uninvite me from the silent watch
I had taken up.

But I keep seeing over and over again
the bird
and the man
regarding each other
and flying away.

For B. V.

The Atheist Prays

I am praying again
and how does one pray
    when unsure if anything hears?

In the world I know as reliable and finite
    when time and matter cycle back and forth
    and I understand the answers to so many puzzles
there are moments when knowing is nothing
and I
    this accumulation of systems, histories
    repetitions falls from me—
    how does one who is sure there is nothing
    pray?
I
dark gathered around my eyes
sit in this room cluttered with my certainties
asking
my one unanswered question
holding myself perfectly still to listen
fixing my gaze
just here

wondering.

Dear Crazy, Crying Heart

Oh, my heart
dear foolish one,
sweet crazy keening heart—

Get ready—hush—
let the winds sweep clean the hidden corners of your lies
Stop crying and wrap your arms
around that child in there
the one in the crash helmet
the one with the broken leg
the baby in the dark
the one with the broken heart
the baby knowing its hand for the first time
the child full of milk and lullabies
the child with not enough food in its belly

It is all God
It is all God
the food   the baby   the hunger
the starfish hand with translucent fingertips
the wrinkles of your face
the memories of seventy years
and knowing your wholeness at another's touch

the brokenness
the cry at the bottom of the mine
the song from the top of the tree

All God, All God

all pouring itself out
for you, heart
dear crazy crying heart
hush

listen to your song.   Ah. Amen.

Remembering My Dad

This sketchy diary
of forgetting and remembering
is of Alzheimers but also
a picture of how far I apprehend
my own forming
by forces that existed for themselves
but also molded me
    in their power
    in their
bumping me holding me thrusting me away
seeing and not seeing me
needing and not saying thank you
saying thank you and meaning
"Be perfectly conformed
    to my idea
    of a child."

I see you sideways
intent upon some task
showing me always your profile in busyness

then I remember
the elevator door sliding
sliding soundlessly across your goodbye
the sorrow in your face
you lie on your bed in the nursing home
small in the dark, forgetting your life

    (and we, too, out here,

    forgetting the life we had with you)
And sorrow overwhelms my healing heart
All the grief from everything else
comes from God knows where
fluttering to this place
I am surrounded.

This morning
every memory about you is grief.

Psalm for Sorrow

I have not understood, perhaps
because death, the thief,
batters this one and that one
before taking them away.
I must, in surrender, ask

Who are you who demands such prices?
Who are you
who tortures meaning from us?

Where are you, hidden
behind this dark curtain,
accused of omnipotence, and more, of irrelevance?

But if you are the friend dying with AIDS,
the old man yielding his body to cancer,
the child with laughter choked in her throat,

And if you abide
in the smallest places
    cupped in the nurse's hand
    giving medication for pain

gathered into the briefest glance
between my brother and his friend
filling all the space between their fingers touching . . .

Let me ask no more
but come   You   hurry
and let me go touch someone.

For Belletini.

BLESSING

We spend so much time running from ourselves
fleeing from what we know
about the goodness in our hearts
we think we can escape
the intelligence of our loving.

Imagine
you are standing before a bodhisattva—
Jesus, Buddha, the first mother
it does not matter what you call the holy one—
he has dust on his shoes
chaff clings to her
the smells of being alive—
Shining from their faces is the beam of
all their questions
the compassion of their living

Can you see yourself through those eyes?
Can we know each other like this?
(We, who no longer believe in messiahs
can hardly believe in each other.)

Can we
know ourselves seen
and know each other this same way
until our restless hearts
learn to abide
in this knowing and this love?
Can we live in this gaze of blessing?

Incarnation

Watching in the morning
for whatever opens to you
when dawn comes pipping through
the egg of the sky
You forget:

something is also waiting for you.

It is not important
that you believe this

(grip it hard through the sullen nights
as an amulet against all bitter days)

only that you remember it
when one day
someone comes sighing your name
arms open in welcome.

PLANTING BURNING BUSHES I

Digging holes for planting
I become intimate with stones
The inevitable scrape of shovel
on the side of a rock
measuring its scope and size.

And if I can move it, if
it is not the ledge supporting this house
I ease my fingers around its gritty flanks
pry up its tossed shape
lift the weight of its beginnings
the ground wet with years of sleeping
a cool baptism of the work of my hands
For a moment
I am goddess of the stone
lifting it into light it has never seen.

Planting Burning Bushes II

My well-planned strategy for a straight hedge
degenerates
I plant where the ledge is not
Where the big rocks are not.

And I never know until I dig
far enough below the surface
What obstacles are there
what rocks
    what old tossed glacial memories
    of origins and slide
    have come to rest
    here
Where one day
I know a burning bush
will sink its roots down
shoot its branches up

house for the voices of birds
shelter for a nest of visions.

WALKING THE DOG AT NIGHT

Because the young black men and I
usually walk around each other
walk wide and wary
muttering greetings
maneuvering through sidewalk space
thick with afterimages of sadness, fear, and
something forgotten but palpable
like wishing it was okay to talk to each other
or not

Because of all this—
when the young man approaches,
sees my ten-year-old terrier seeing him
wagging, waiting for him,
the young man smiling, walking by and
walking on by backward looking some more
and, looking, says to me:
"I like his eyes,"

I feel the thickness dissolve,
and imagine the air cleansed—
a young black man smiling at my old dog
and this middle-aged white woman

liking this man's eyes, too,
I want this moment to go on
and on becoming what it wants to become
filling the now narrow space between us
with all that is possible.

In Brasov, Piaţa Sfatului

The moment comes and goes so fast.
So often we are called for and not ready.
"Jesus is Lord"
the old beggar whispers
at the locked door of the orthodox church.
Practiced in English it is a lesson
beseeching rich travelers
who seek old icons.

Theologies flit through my mind
and warnings against beggars—
     give to one and you will be surrounded—
"Yaysoos ees lord," he says.
Not mine.
No matter.

The money in my pocket
might have got him bread for a week.

I had it.
I did not give it.
I am surrounded anyway—

The lessons—
    how want looks in any language;
    how far and close the distance
        between having much and having not enough;
    how crucial the moment when we are called to know
        the yeast of Christ's communion bread is now
        in our hands
        to keep or knead into new food—

these lessons are not about theology
or money

but bread

bread again
and, once again, bread.

For Nagy Bela.

In Medias/Medgyes

I.   I have been warned
that when we cross from Old Romania
into Transylvania
to join our people there
we should use Hungarian place names
not Romanian (say Kolozsvar, not Cluj).
Old enmities maintain old boundaries
depending on which history troubles whom.

Yet, at this table, we strangers
lingering over coffee and sweets
are slipping back and forth among three languages,
sometimes translating
sometimes hearing with our hearts.

II.   And remembering my childhood,
I find something in this that has less to do with
the sounds of my grandparents' voices
that come back to me and speak through my mouth
    fata frumosa
    taç, si mînca
    draga, micuţa

> *fi cu minte*
> *draga*
> less to do with memory
> than with these good people now
> and another return
> to the home in the heart.

III. History is going on
armies continue to arm
victims everywhere take their places.
And, by the light of our matches and cigarettes,
faith in life whispers across the borders.

For Kiss Karoly and Kiss Ana.

fata frumosa	pretty little girl
taç, si mînca	hush, and eat
draga, micuţa	dear little one
fi cu minte	be polite
draga	dear one

LOVE ABIDES

Often we are found in our grief and comforted
    calmed by some kindness
    brought alive again by beauty
    that catches us undefended.

Even when the sun is most thin and far
even at the hour the storm is at its height
we can go through
    renewal nests within sorrow
    love abides, even beyond anger, beyond death.

We are held in an embrace invisible but infinite
moving with all creation
between wholeness and fragmentation
moving always toward the one.

Small joys and great sorrows pass
and we, with steps uncertain, move on
to whatever is next

but continually seen, heard, held
by Life infinite and remote, intimate and abiding.

Love, do not let us go.   Amen.

PRAYER ON SUNDAY MORNING

1. Dawn rose from the lake while I slept
There are no monks here
   to ride four-mile winds on kites of praise,
no priests leaning into the howling gaps
   to set prayer wheels spinning.
Here there are no gaps
where prayer flags snap
in the same breath of whatever utters
the beginnings of mountains.

Buddha does not require praise, nor the Tao,
nor the great unnameable God
toward whom we turn our backs.
The minotaur does not prowl anymore
for its breakfast of virgins.
   No deity demands prayers anymore—
   powerless to answer petitions
   gods wait to be released between us
   through our hands.

It is I who need to light candles
Pray (breathe words like flames)

    my silences alight in my blank face
Ride what rises on my warm breath, ride it out past dawn.

II. Here (not in Lhasa, nor Rome, nor anywhere
      holy, magnificent, and far)
here day wakes with the drone of buses warming up
Plastic grocery bags caught in the branches
my prayer flags
    accidental, filling and collapsing
    in the breath between apartment buildings
    with sighs and curses in a hundred languages
snapping and twisting with the 10,000 names of the
      unnameable.

I, half believing in the dawn,
write prayers in the half light
prayers for my people and my times
filling and collapsing in our internal breezes
and listen for some encouragement to go
where I must.

REUNION

One of the old ones stood up
into the morning light
and spoke to those who had come
back to the river.

—Now we have come again to this place.
My life apart from you
is not as strong.
Yes,
I have danced and
I have told the stories
at my own fire and
I have sung well, to all eight directions.

But when I am with you,
my friends,
I know better
who it is in me
that sings.

SHORT SUTRA

It never gets easier.
Paying attention to my breath
my impatience becomes quiet
    only by continual practice
I am never done noticing how I veer to anger
    never stop needing to turn again with breath and love

I cannot replace old with new
it is love and remembering
seeing and turning
forever

CALL IN THE
STRAIT OF GEORGIA

Each dawn, waiting on my bench,
I called in a whisper, Come.
Unmet for three days and unseen
until the last dawn when
I had grown unfaithful
I had to be told, as the sun rose,
to turn around
to look at that place
where the fingers of foam
slipped under the mist
and for the last time
see the black legs pushing
see the bird lifting itself
casting its whole self
into its other element.

I was bound to the ground the bird had left
bound and abandoned and blessed

And still feel bound
all my objections silenced by a feather
laid across my lips
If I spoke the feather would rise
and be gone with that one word
as that moment is gone.

Nothing remains but this—
no raven with a coal
but a great blue heron rising away asking
Who shall I send?

Send me.

MORNING WATCH

Patiently
we waited in the dark.
The planet turned
and we upon it
stupid with sleep
    hoped something would happen.

While we leaned toward the east
the weight of the night sank behind us,
toward the north a comet passed so close
we could see it through the sleep in our eyes,
and then dawn flung itself up
swirling with clouds and color and birdsong.

Look—this is our world for another day.
Reach out to it, it is your own life.
Know, too, that this day is dear
even to strangers you will never know.
Stretch out your arms to embrace it.

Do not go back to sleep.

For Harry Scholefield.

Unitarian Universalist
Meditation Manuals

This list includes all meditation manuals since the merger in 1961. For information about meditations prior to 1961, contact Skinner House Books, 25 Beacon Street, Boston, MA 02108.

1999   *The Rock of Ages at the Taj Mahal* Meg Barnhouse
       Morning Watch Barbara Pescan
1998   *Glory, Hallelujah! Now Please Pick Up Your Socks*
              Jane Ellen Mauldin
       Evening Tide Elizabeth Tarbox
1997   *A Temporary State of Grace* David S. Blanchard
       Green Mountain Spring and Other Leaps of Faith
              Gary A. Kowalski
1996   *Taking Pictures of God* Bruce T. Marshall
       Blessing the Bread Lynn Ungar
1995   *In the Holy Quiet of This Hour* Richard S. Gilbert
1994   *In the Simple Morning Light* Barbara Rohde
1993   *Life Tides* Elizabeth Tarbox
       The Gospel of Universalism Tom Owen-Towle
1992   *Noisy Stones* Robert R. Walsh
1991   *Been in the Storm So Long* Mark Morrison-Reed
              and Jacqui James, Editors
1990   *Into the Wilderness* Sara Moores Campbell
1989   *A Small Heaven* Jane Ranney Rzepka
1988   *The Numbering of Our Days* Anthony Friess Perrino

Morning Watch

MEDITATIONS BY Barbara Pescan

"I brought *Morning Watch* with me to a café and began to read. The very first poem I turned to moved me to tears. The man at the next table asked me if something was wrong. No, I said, everything was right, but I was very affected by a friend's poem. He asked if he could read it—soon this complete stranger also began to weep. This is a numinous book that makes the English language sing like it ought to."
> —The Reverend Mark Belletini, First Unitarian Universalist Church, Columbus, Ohio

"Barbara Pescan's poems touch deeply and sing with earth-life. Her work gives voice to religious community."
> —Carol Hepokoski, Professor of Religious Ethics, Meadville/Lombard Theological School

"Barbara Pescan writes from her heart, painting from her palette of words and brushing in an occasional handful of gravel. Her poems are beautifully, skillfully crafted. Keep them by your side and read them often."
> —Roz Reynolds, lifelong Unitarian and current member of the Church of the Larger Fellowship

A Unitarian Universalist since her teens, **Barbara Pescan** attended the UU Church of Akron, Ohio, where her mother, sister and nephew still are active. Since 1995, she has shared the senior minister position at the Unitarian Church of Evanston, Illinois, with her partner, Ann Tyndall. Her poems have appeared in *Singing the Living Tradition, First Days Record* and the *Journal of Liberal Religious Response.*

Skinner House Books
Unitarian Universalist Association
25 Beacon Street
Boston, MA 02108-2800

ISBN 1-55896-376-6

DYING OUT LOUD

JOURNAL

A 28-Day Prayer Challenge

MIKE MURRAY